Date: 5/27/16

J 973 MUR
Murray, Julie,
United States /

UNITED STATES

Big Buddy Books

An Imprint of Abdo Publishing
abdopublishing.com

Julie Murray

abdopublishing.com

Published by Abdo Publishing, a division of ABDO, PO Box 398166, Minneapolis, Minnesota 55439.
Copyright © 2016 by Abdo Consulting Group, Inc. International copyrights reserved in all countries. No part
of this book may be reproduced in any form without written permission from the publisher. Big Buddy Books™
is a trademark and logo of Abdo Publishing.

Printed in the United States of America, North Mankato, Minnesota.
092015
012016

THIS BOOK CONTAINS
RECYCLED MATERIALS

Cover Photo: Shutterstock.com.
Interior Photos: ASSOCIATED PRESS (pp. 15, 17, 27); Nancy Carter/North Wind Picture Archives (p. 15);
    Glow Images (p. 33); Leon Halip/Getty Images (p. 27); © iStockphoto.com (pp. 11, 16, 25, 34, 35, 38);
    Lenorlux/Deposit Photos (p. 13); Michael Ochs Archives/Getty Images (p. 31); Oxford Science Archive/
    Glow Images (p. 33); Shutterstock.com (pp. 5, 9, 11, 19, 21, 23, 29, 34, 35, 37, 38); Justin Sullivan/Getty
    Images (p. 19); © Jim Zuckerman/CORBIS/Glow Images (p. 35).

Coordinating Series Editor: Megan M. Gunderson
Editor: Katie Lajiness
Contributing Editors: Bridget O'Brien, Marcia Zappa
Graphic Design: Adam Craven

Country population and area figures taken from the CIA World Factbook.

Library of Congress Cataloging-in-Publication Data

Murray, Julie, 1969-
  United States / Julie Murray.
      pages cm. -- (Explore the countries (set 3))
  Includes index.
  ISBN 978-1-68078-072-7
1. United States--Juvenile literature. I. Title.
  E178.3.M96 2016
  973--dc23
                        2015023795

UNITED STATES

CONTENTS

AROUND THE WORLD

Our world has many countries. Each country has beautiful land. It has its own rich history. And, the people have their own languages and ways of life.

The United States (US) is a country in North America. What do you know about the United States? Let's learn more about this place and its story!

Did You Know?

There is no official language in the United States.

The Statue of Liberty is a famous monument in New York City, New York. France gifted it to the United States in 1884. To many, it is a symbol of freedom.

5

PASSPORT TO THE UNITED STATES

The United States is mostly in the middle of North America. Canada is to the north and Mexico is to the south. The Pacific Ocean is to the west and the Atlantic Ocean is to the east.

The United States is split into 50 states. Only 48 states are connected. Alaska borders northwestern Canada. Hawaii is a group of islands in the Pacific.

The total area of the United States is 3,794,100 square miles (9,826,675 sq km). About 321 million people live there.

WHERE IN THE WORLD?

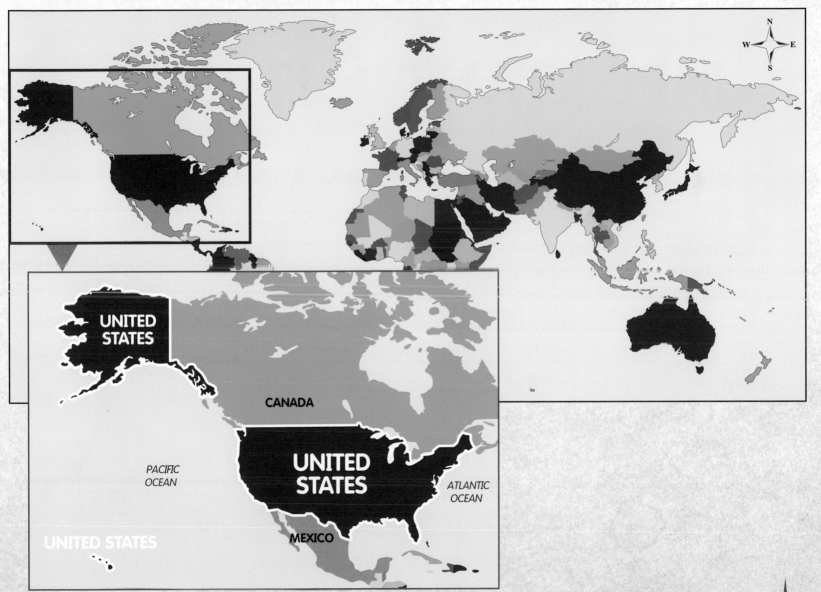

IMPORTANT CITIES

Washington, DC, is the US **capital**. About 600,000 people live in the city. About 5.6 million people live in the surrounding area.

Washington, DC, is the only city in the country that is not part of a state. Instead, it makes up a special district called the District of Columbia. The city is known for its importance to politics and government. It has many national monuments.

New York City, New York, is the country's largest city. More than 8 million people live there. Almost 19 million people live in the surrounding area. New York City is made up of five large areas called boroughs. New York City is known for its art and food.

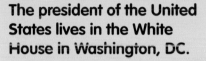

The president of the United States lives in the White House in Washington, DC.

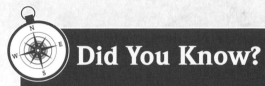

UNITED STATES

New York
Chicago
Washington, DC
Los Angeles

SAY IT

boroughs
BUHR-ohs

Broadway is a street in New York City. Many people come to the Broadway area to see shows with singing and dancing.

Los Angeles, California, is the second-largest city in the United States. It is home to about 3.8 million people. About 12.8 million people live in the surrounding area.

The Hollywood area of Los Angeles is known for making movies. Many movie stars live near there.

Chicago, Illinois, is the third-largest city in the United States. Nearly 2.7 million people live in the city. Chicago is located on the banks of Lake Michigan. The city is known as a large producer of metal products, foods, and other goods.

The names of famous people are written on stars in the sidewalks in Hollywood.

Chicago's Willis Tower (*right*) is one of the world's tallest buildings. With 110 stories, it is 1,450 feet (442 m) tall.

United States in History

Europeans began traveling to North America during the late 1400s. They met **Native Americans**. Native Americans taught the travelers about new foods. These included corn and squash.

Great Britain formed 13 colonies in what is now the United States. Virginia was the first colony. It was built in 1607. Later, the colonies won freedom from Great Britain's government and taxes.

Did You Know?

Native Americans lived in the Americas for thousands of years before Europeans arrived. European settlement changed the Native American way of life forever.

Native Americans taught the settlers how to travel by canoe. A canoe is a light, narrow boat.

SAY IT

Canoe
kuh-NOO

In 1803, the United States agreed to buy 828,000 square miles (2,145,000 sq km) of North American land from the French. This is known as the Louisiana Purchase. Over time, this land became all or parts of 15 states.

From 1861 to 1865, the United States fought a **civil war**. The Northern states defeated the South. The United States remained whole.

The Great Depression was a sad time for most Americans. From 1929 to about 1939, many lost their jobs and homes and went hungry. After **World War II**, the country prospered again.

In August 2005, Hurricane Katrina destroyed New Orleans, Louisiana. This storm was very powerful. More than 1,800 people died.

During the Great Depression, many hungry people waited in long, crowded breadlines for hours. Each person received little food even after the long wait.

From 1804 to 1806, Meriwether Lewis and William Clark explored the Louisiana Purchase and beyond. They made maps and met Native Americans. They also collected information about plants and animals.

TIMELINE

1776

On July 4, the Declaration of Independence was adopted. It announced that the United States was separate from Great Britain.

1920

Women won the right to vote. The women who fought for this right were known as suffragettes.

1861–1865

The American **Civil War** was fought between the South and the North. From 1860 to 1861, 11 Southern states left the United States. They wanted their own country and to own **slaves**. The North wanted to keep the country together and end slavery. The North won the war.

1941

On December 7, Japanese military forces attacked Pearl Harbor in Hawaii. This attack brought the United States into **World War II**.

2001

On September 11, four aircraft were stolen while in the air. Three planes flew into buildings. The fourth crashed in a field. The World Trade Center towers in New York City were destroyed. Part of the Pentagon, near Washington, DC, was also ruined. About 3,000 people were killed.

2008

Barack Obama became the first African American elected president of the United States.

An Important Symbol

The US flag has 50 stars. Each star represents one state. The stripes change from red to white. There are 7 red and 6 white stripes. The 13 stripes stand for the original 13 colonies.

The US government is a **federal republic**. Power is shared among different parts of the government. The United States is also a democracy. In a democracy, people vote on how to run their country.

The first official US flag was made in 1777. It had 13 stars. More stars were added as more states joined the country.

Barack Obama was elected president for a second time in 2012. Presidents can serve two terms.

ACROSS THE LAND

The United States has many different types of land. It ranges from the arctic to the desert and from the flatlands to the mountains.

Alaska is the largest state. It has thousands of **glaciers**. Denali is in Alaska. At about 20,300 feet (6,200 m), it is the highest mountain in North America.

Did You Know?

Temperatures in the United States have a broad range. In North Dakota, the summer record high is 121°F (49°C). The winter record low is -60°F (-51°C).

Juneau is the capital of Alaska. It is located between water and mountains, so no roads have been built leading to the city. People must take a boat or an airplane to travel there.

SAY IT

Juneau
JOO-noh

The Great Basin is a large desert area in the western United States. It covers about 200,000 square miles (520,000 sq km).

The United States is home to many types of animals. Coyotes, lizards, hawks, and rabbits live in the deserts. Bison, foxes, gophers, and spiders live in the plains.

Many different plants grow in the United States. Spruce, willow, and poplar trees grow in the northern states. Oak, palmetto, and magnolia trees are common in the south. About 25,000 types of flowers grow in the United States!

The Great Basin's lowest point is Death Valley in California. Thousands of years ago, this desert was a lake!

Earning a Living

The United States provides many goods and services. Some people make things such as cars, computers, and food. Others work for the government. They might be police officers or work in a courtroom.

Many people in the United States have service jobs. They might work in banking, law, or health care. Or, they might have jobs helping visitors in places such as hotels or coffeehouses.

Farmers in the United States grow crops and raise livestock on the country's rich land. Beef cattle and corn are two popular farm products.

Some farmers raise cows for dairy foods. Many dairy farms are in California, Wisconsin (*below*), New York, Pennsylvania, and Idaho.

LIFE IN THE UNITED STATES

The United States is a modern country. Yet, it is also known for its history and natural beauty.

Today, many people travel to the United States. They want to see its art and fashion. Many people want to taste American food. Popular American foods include cheeseburgers, pizza, fried chicken, and hot dogs.

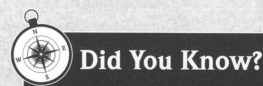

Did You Know?

In the United States, education standards are different in every state. Children must attend school starting around age 6. Most children receive at least 13 years of education.

Many Americans eat hot dogs at baseball games. Baseball is so popular it is known as the national pastime.

American artist Andy Warhol made art known as Pop Art. It was based on common objects such as soup cans.

SAY IT

Warhol
WAR-hall

27

The United States is famous for American football. It is one of the country's most popular sports. The National Football League (NFL) started in 1920. It has 32 teams. The biggest NFL game of the year is called the Super Bowl.

Faith is important in the United States. About 75 percent of all Americans are **Christian**. Others are **Jewish**, **Muslim**, or another belief.

Did You Know?

The first Olympics in the United States were held in Saint Louis, Missouri, in 1904. Americans won more than 230 medals.

The Chapel of San Miguel is in Santa Fe, New Mexico. It is one of the oldest Christian churches in the United States. It was built around 1620. It has been rebuilt many times over the years.

Famous Faces

Many famous people are from the United States. Martin Luther King Jr. was born on January 15, 1929. He was an important **civil rights movement** leader. King fought for the rights of African Americans and other people.

King gave well-known speeches. His "I Have a Dream" speech is his most famous. King gave this speech in Washington, DC, in 1963.

King was shot and killed on April 4, 1968. His birthday is honored as a national holiday on the third Monday in January.

King won the 1964 Nobel Peace Prize for his peaceful marches. Nobel Prizes are awarded each year in six categories for outstanding accomplishments.

Neil Armstrong was born on August 5, 1930. He went on his first space flight in 1966.

Armstrong joined the Apollo 11 team for his second trip to space. On July 20, 1969, he became the first person to walk on the moon. Armstrong is famous for saying, "That's one small step for a man, one giant leap for mankind."

Armstrong took photos on the moon. He also collected moon rocks to bring back to Earth.

Armstrong (*left*) went to the moon and back with Michael Collins (*center*) and Buzz Aldrin (*right*) on Apollo 11.

SAY IT

Apollo
uh-PAH-loh

TOUR BOOK

Imagine traveling to the United States! Here are some places you could go and things you could do.

 ## Sing

Sing "Take Me Out to the Ballgame" at a Major League Baseball game! There are 30 teams around the country. The Chicago Cubs play at Wrigley Field in Chicago.

Celebrate

Thanksgiving Day is a holiday on the fourth Thursday in November. People give thanks for what they have. Many people eat turkey with mashed potatoes and gravy.

 ## See

Disneyland is a fun park in Anaheim, California. There are rides, food, and characters from Disney movies.

 ## Explore

Yellowstone National Park is the oldest national park in the world. Walk through hundreds of miles of trails. See bears, elk, and bald eagles in the wild.

 ## Taste

Try Bassett Ice Cream in Philadelphia, Pennsylvania. It has been a family-owned business since 1861! Taste flavors like banana or cookies and cream.

A Great Country

The story of the United States is important to our world. The United States is a land of towering mountains and wide plains. It is a country of strong people with new ideas.

The people and places that make up the United States offer something special. They help make the world a more beautiful, interesting place.

Lake Superior is one of the world's largest freshwater lakes. It is also the largest of the five Great Lakes. The Great Lakes are a group of lakes in the United States and Canada.

SAY IT

Superior
su-PIHR-ee-uhr

United States Up Close

Official Name: United States of America

Flag:

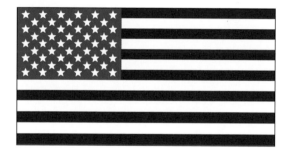

Population (rank): 321,368,864
(July 2015 est.)
(fourth most-populated country)

Total Area (rank): 3,794,100 square miles
(third largest country)

Capital: Washington, DC

Official Language: No official language

Currency: US dollar

Form of Government: Federal republic

National Anthem: "The Star-Spangled Banner"

IMPORTANT WORDS

capital a city where government leaders meet.

Christian (KRIHS-chuhn) a person who practices Christianity, which is a religion that follows the teachings of Jesus Christ.

civil rights movement the public fight for civil rights for all citizens. Civil rights include the right to vote and freedom of speech.

civil war a war between groups in the same country.

federal republic a form of government in which the people choose the leader. The central government and the individual states share power.

glacier (GLAY-shuhr) a huge chunk of ice and snow on land.

Jewish a person who practices Judaism, which is a religion based on laws recorded in the Torah, or is related to the ancient Hebrews.

Muslim a person who practices Islam, which is a religion based on a belief in Allah as God and Muhammad as his prophet.

Native Americans the very first people who lived in America.

slavery the practice of owning people as slaves. A slave is a person who is bought and sold as property.

World War II a war fought in Europe, Asia, and Africa from 1939 to 1945.

WEBSITES

To learn more about Explore the Countries, visit **booklinks.abdopublishing.com**. These links are routinely monitored and updated to provide the most current information available.

INDEX